By the Best-Se...
1066 and All That

AND NOW ALL THIS

In this hilarious geographical, ornothological,
mythological and what-have-you
follow-up to
1066 and All That,
MESSRS SELLAR AND YEATMAN
once again proved
that a little learning is a humorous thing.
The proof stands.

Your thanks are due to the Vice-Proctor of the Hole Pocket University for insisting on the bathing costumes; and to Mr. John Reynolds for kindly leaving this Maddening Symbolical Design unfinished.